Cape Cod Blessings,

Carol Hamblet Adams

The Gift of Cape Cod

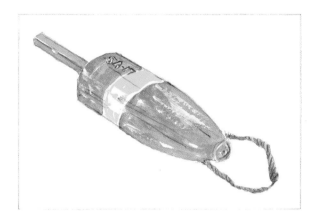

by Carol Hamblet Adams

Original Illustrations by Bobbie Wilkinson

broken shell
PRESS

The Gift of Cape Cod

Text copyright © 2010 by Carol Hamblet Adams
Published by Broken Shell Press
Brewster, MA 02631
www.brokenshellpress.com

ISBN 978-0-615-28792-8

Book Design by Adams Litke Design Co., Seattle, WA 98115
www.adamslitkedesign.com

Printed in the USA

Acknowledgments

A great big "thank you" to my twin sister, Bobbie Wilkinson, for her beautiful illustrations and to my daughter, Kristin Adams Litke, for her wonderful graphic design. This book would never have been possible without their invaluable help.

Dedication

In memory of my beloved husband and best friend, Steve, who shared so many cherished moments with me on Cape Cod.

To my greatest blessings, Kristin and Mike, Amanda and Kevin, Rogers and Eamon, Maura and Todd. You are the lights of my life. Here's to many more fun-filled family reunions and treasured memories on beautiful Cape Cod.

And to God, Who brought me to Cape Cod... and Who guides me... inspires me... and supports me every day of my life.

Preface

I have been coming to Cape Cod for many years and am blessed to live here now. I am so grateful for the peace and serenity I find here and for all the gifts the Cape has to offer. I hope this little book will keep the magic of beautiful Cape Cod alive in your heart forever.

With love,

Carol

 ... Beside restful waters He leads me;
He refreshes my soul.

Psalm 23:2-3

To: _____

From: _____

Thank You, God,
for the gift of
Cape Cod.

For its sandy, white beaches
and the smell of rich, salt air

wind-swept dunes and
weathered beach fences

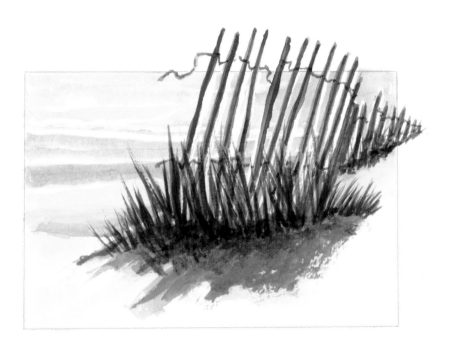

seagulls

graceful shore birds

ocean waves crashing against the coast

the ebb and flow of the tides

sun-drenched days

bright beach umbrellas

sandcastles built with dreams

hydrangeas blooming everywhere

sandpails and shovels

kites that soar in the sky

flip-flops

the smell of suntan lotion

the fun of summer barbeques

good books

sand between my toes

outdoor showers

beautiful shells

beach stones

the unexpected gift of sea glass

low tide on Cape Cod Bay

tidepools filled with surprises

hermit crabs

a stray buoy washed up
on the shore

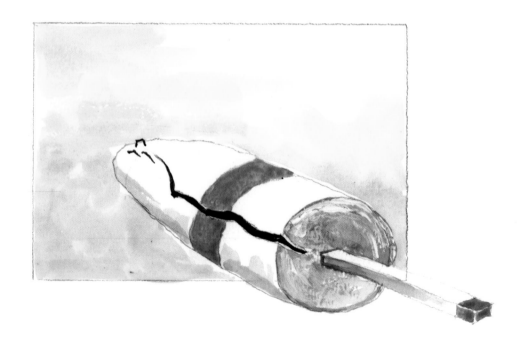

majestic lighthouses
still guarding our coast

harbors dotted with vessels
of every shape and size

colorful canoes and kayaks that
glide gracefully over our waters

winding bike paths

lush, green golf courses

band concerts

baseball games

the laughter of children

cranberry bogs

lobster rolls and clam shacks

ice cream cones

off-roading adventures

the wonder of herring runs

gift shops

art galleries

saltwater taffy

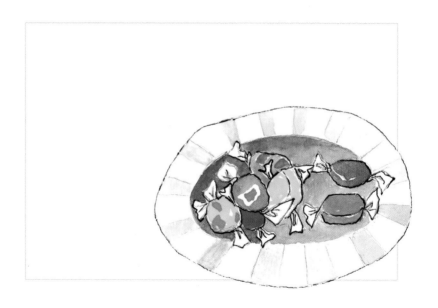

fishing boats that break the silence
of the early morning

ferry boat rides to Martha's Vineyard and Nantucket

seals playing in the ocean waves

whale watching

brilliant sunrises

and the magic of an evening sunset.

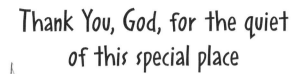

Thank You, God, for the quiet
of this special place

where I leave my cares behind
and appreciate each moment.

Thank You for solitude

for time spent with loved ones

and a chance to reflect on my blessings.

Thank You for treasured
family and friends

for this sacred place where simplicity reigns

and cherished memories last a lifetime.

Thank You, God, for the gift of Cape Cod. May its peace remain in my heart forever.

About the Author

Carol Hamblet Adams is a motivational speaker and the author of "My Beautiful Broken Shell: Words of Hope to Refresh the Soul". Carol's life centers around her faith, family, friends and God's magnificent seashore. She lives on beautiful Cape Cod and can be found beachcombing on its sandy shores or swimming in its blue-green waters. Carol can be reached at carolhambletadams@comcast.net or www.carolhambletadams.com.

About the Illustrator

Bobbie Wilkinson is a musician, writer and artist, who illustrated the original version of "My Beautiful Broken Shell". Her passions include her faith, her family, her rescued cocker spaniel, the seashore and the Virginia countryside she and her husband call home. Bobbie created "The Flip-Flop Heart"© line of jewelry, artwork and greeting cards that can be seen at her website: www.theflipflopheart.com.

A percentage of the profits from this book will be donated to Dana-Farber Cancer Institute in Boston to help fund lymphoma research in memory of Carol's husband, Steve.